To Little Yongi, with Immense Love

Rosângela de Fátima Sviercoski

Second Edition

To Little Yongi, with Immense Love

ISBN: 978-619-91356-6-2

To Little Yongi, with Immense Love

Rosângela de Fátima Sviercoski

illustrations: Vesela Kucheva

Sofia, 2022

Little panda Yongi lived happily with his mother Yongiedoma in a beautiful city on the Black Sea Coast of Bulgaria. There they played together in the parks and swam on the beaches!

Yongi was a very special panda who was gifted with so much love that he had to have two hearts. Besides his mother Yongiedoma, Yongi really loved his older brother Edo. Edo lived far away because he was studying at university, but often he would visit his beloved family. When they would unite, they all played together in as many different ways, as Yongiedoma could think of.

They loved to sing and dance together with music from „Little Spotted Chicken" and „Words in Songs". Together they used to sing "Our Father" and also to pray: „Thank you, God, our Father, because we have food, we are healthy and we are together! Bless also Edo!"

VRAS
CANTADAS

Do you know what they liked to play together the most!? They loved to play „Five little monkeys jumping on the bed", „Frog Jaburana" and also to pretend to be dinosaurs... They also loved to read the „Book of Numbers", and the book for the little white rabbit Flopsi, as well as many other books.

They played a game called *Kung-Fu Panda*, where Yongi would climb on the back of the mother, who would pretend to be a „little horse", after that they would all fall and start a joyful fight! At other times, Yongi would hold tight on the legs of his mother while she walked, pretending to be a koala, instead of a little lovely panda with a black rectangle around the eyes…

Yongiedoma loves all sorts of games, arts and projects that involves Mathematics. That is why she would also create many interesting mathematical games to play together.

But, one day, while in kindergarten, Yongi was kidnapped and taken far away from Yongiedoma. The two happy hearts of the little panda were now filled with sadness. Just as the joy and love had been doubled, now Yongi's sadness became doubled by being taken away.

When she learned that Yongi would not come home, Yongiedoma rushed to seek help to find Yongi. So she found out that the little panda with the two hearts already lives in a distant city, and only the strongest and most courageous creature can bring Yongi back to her. But what is this creature and where to find it?

Yongi was taken far away in a city at the foot of the mountains. There the little panda had a new home, new friends, but with this abrupt change the little one needed to learn how not to show how much he misses the mother Yongiedoma and the suffering he was feeling from this sad separation.

Yongiedoma also went away to the distant city and asked everyone she met, not knowing how to find her child! Finally, she had no choice, but to came to the big city and live there without Yongi!

АСП
ДСИ
ДАЗ
РПУ
ПЯТЕТЯ

Yongiedoma had no help neither from the animals, nor from the people responsible for order and tranquility in the city. Look at how many different institutions she went almost every day seeking help!

All the ones she met only complained against the system, pretend they are horrified and put their hands on their heads, but not on their hearts, and did nothing to get Yongi back to his mother! Because they simply do not think neither like mothers nor like children!

But, the sad and lonely mother still found many good friends who were willing to help her not to lose hope to get her child back! Because of that, Yongiedoma has not given up, and until this day, she continues to look for the „responsible people or animals" who will help her to be together with her child. Until now no institution had helped her, simply because they do not want to waste time and power, they have more important things to do!

Almost four years had passed and Yongi now has to pretend that he does not want to talk or even to hug his own mother. How could Yongi become like that?

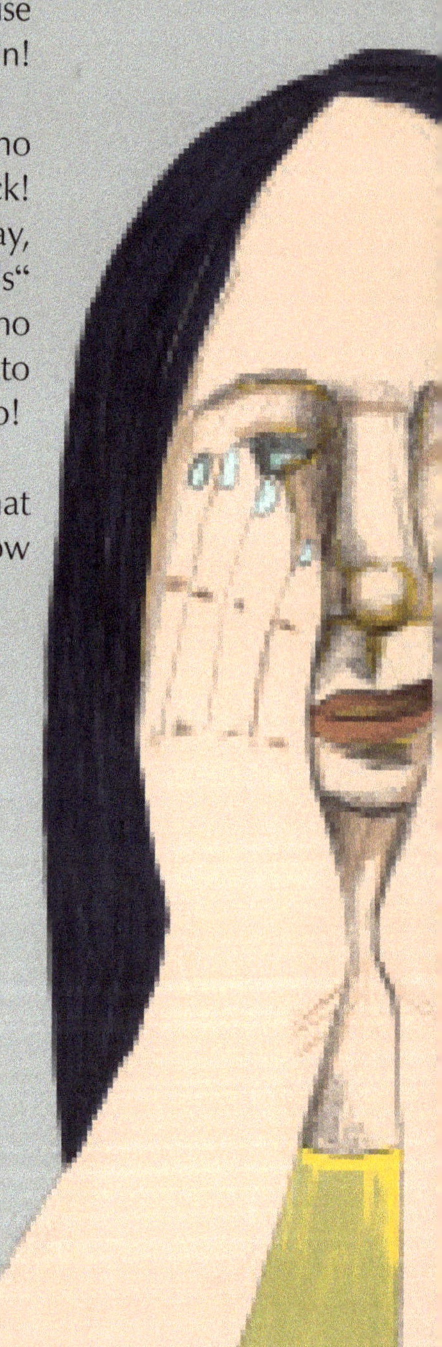

Still, Yongiedoma has faith that she will meet the strongest and most brave creature to reunite her with her child. Every day she prays to God for His guidance and also with other mothers, and awaits the day Yongie will return home.

Draw for yourself an image for the end of this story. What does this strongest creature that can help Yongiedoma and Yongi to be together again, look like?

Afterword:

Dear parents,

The story of the little panda Yongi is dedicated to the two children of the author, Yoan and Angelina (Angie). The name is a combination of both (Yo(a)ngi), ommiting the "a". After their parents divorced in 2012, the father took them secretly in 2015, and although the court pronounced several times in favor of the mother, none of the responsible institutions have so far committed themselves to returning them to her. In the struggle to see and be with her children, the mother has only being assisted in rare and brief encounters with them. During almost **seven years**, she has seen them few times, always in the presence of social workers and in closed doors inside institutions. For the last seven years, rarely she played with them and huged them! She never could participate on their birthdays or spend holiday together.

Specialists have found out that Yoan and Angelina are victims of the so-called „Syndrome of Parental Alienation" a term by which psychologists call the child's psychological trauma when one parent deliberately hinders contact with the other and sets the children against the left behind parent. The consequences of this trauma for the child can be severe and long-term - low self-esteem and self-image, depression, developmental disturbances. **Unfortunately, these cases are very common in Bulgaria, with estimates being around 16,000 ongoing children suffering.**

These are the institutions, illustrated in the book, where the mother has sought help without success and some she still seeks help until this day:

РПУ (RPU) - Police Units in the cities of Sofia, Kostinbrod and Godetch.
ОЗД (OZD) - Social Service Unit – Lozenetz and Svoge (Godetch).
ЦОПП-КБ (TSOP-KB) - Center for social Assistance in Kostinbrod.
АСП (ACP) - Social Service of Bulgaria.
ДАЗД (DAZD) - National Agency for Child Protection.

СъД-КБ (SAD-KB) - Court in Kostinbrod.
ФПП (FPP) - Foundation for Psychological Help, owned by Ms. Galina Kubratova
ЕСПА (ESPA) - Private school in Sofia owned by Ms. Elena K. Nemtsova-Spasova and directed by Ms. Irena Milusheva.
ПАТЕТА (PATETA) - Private Kindergarten in Sofia owned by Ms. Velika Angelova Vasileva and directed by Ms. Anita Vasileva
ЧСИ и ДСИ (**14 Bailiffs**) - K. Darov, M. Tsacheva, V. Tsachev, P. Slavov, M. Stoyanova, R. Milcheva, M. Tsacheva, G. Dichev, M. Bazinski, P. Spasov, V. Xristova, M. Stoyanova, N. Kovacheva, M. Stoyanova.

By purchasing this book **you will be part of an awareness campaign on this ongoing social crisis in the country. The profits will be use to support initiatives to establish programs of prevention.**

About the author:

The author is a Brazilian citizen who came to Bulgaria to work on an EU project through the prestigious Marie Curie International Fellowship. Before that, she worked in the USA where she received permanent residency under the category of National Interest Waiver. She is now an Associate Professor in the Bulgarian Academy of Science in the area of Applied Mathematics and Computational Modeling.

Acknowledgments:

The author is really thankful to the donors who already helped to make this book a reality! In particular the donors at the site: https://www.gofundme.com/children039s-book-a-story-on-parental-alienation.

The author is also thankful to Mr. Rumen Stoyanov, for helping in the Bulgarian translation. Also, she has been helped by Ms. Bosilena Melteva on the English edition and the Bulgarian version, as well as all the other staff from the Bulgarian Helsinki Committee for supporting this cause.

Pope Francis

is also reading the story of the

𝕴ittle 𝖄ongi!

To Little Yongi, with Immense Love
Rosangela de Fatima Sviercoski

English. Second Edition

Illustrator
Vesela Kucheva

Pre-press
Rosangla de Fatima Sviercoski

Publisher
Rosangla de Fatima Sviercoski